# Wealth Beyond Taxes

*How Pharmaceutical Professionals Are Using The Tax Code To Their Advantage To Generate More Income and Wealth*

Christopher Lester ChFC®, RICP®, CCPS®

# CONTENTS

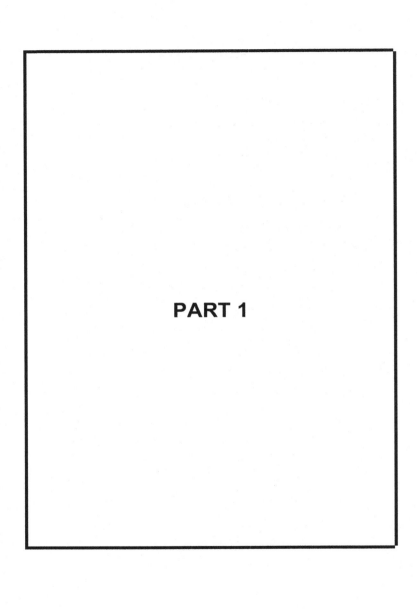

PART 1

**WELCOME**

# WHO SHOULD READ THIS BOOK?

There are two things I want you to know about me right from the start. The first is that as of the day I am writing this, my experience in helping individuals and families with their financial planning is 30 years. I hold the Chartered Financial Consultant (ChFC®), the Retirement Income Certified Professional (RICP®), and the Certified College Planner (CCPS) designations.

The question that I typically get asked as well is, "*Are you a fiduciary?*" And the answer is yes. If you are not already familiar with the term fiduciary let me give you the Reader's Digest version of what that means. I must by law put my clients' interests ahead of my own.

The second thing I'd like you to know about me is that during my 30 years as a financial professional I have worked with a variety of people from all walks of life. But increasingly I discovered that some of my best clients and people that I most enjoy working with are pharmaceutical professionals. New Jersey (which is where I was born and raised) is a hub for the pharmaceutical industry, with many major corporations located here. And as a natural result, I have developed many clients in the industry.

While pharmaceutical professionals may share similar goals and aspirations to folks in other industries, there are specific characteristics of your industry that I have gotten to know intimately. I have become an expert in helping professionals just like you take advantage of all of the options that are available when it comes to using the tax code to pay less in tax, legally, ethically, and morally.

If you are a pharmaceutical professional (a W2 employee, 1099 contractor, or business owner) the Wealth Beyond Taxes strategies outlined in this book can help you pay significantly less in taxes over the course of your lifetime and help you generate more income and wealth for you and your family.

# MY PROMISE TO YOU

If you are still with me, I promise not to waste the next hour or so of your life. Quite the contrary, and I truly hope this book gives you a new option and inspiration when it comes to planning for both your present-day finances and your future retirement.

If you picked up this book then I think I know a few things about you already.

1. **You're not stupid.** Your financial picture may not be as solid as you want it to be, but not because you didn't pay attention. You listened to the experts and did what they advised you to do. You probably consult a financial advisor now, have a CPA do your taxes, and follow the trends in the market.

2. **You're not lazy.** You work hard and earn every penny that comes your way. By

working hard and using your talents, you earn a good living. You will do almost anything it takes to provide for your family and secure their future. I applaud you!

3. **You're not looking for a magic bullet**. Okay, it would be nice if there were some genie in a bottle to grant you the financial well-being you want. (If you find one, feel free to give me a call.) But you're not counting on it or even looking for it. You want the facts and can make up your own mind when presented with those facts.

Anybody who knows me knows I tend to be direct, matter of fact, and detest wasting time. I am a United States Navy veteran and my training in mechanical engineering gives me an inherent ability to problem solve and make complex subjects easy to understand.

I promise to do my part and give you proven and effective strategies to significantly reduce the amount of taxes you'll pay to the government over the course of your lifetime.

# INTRODUCTION

You're probably like most people who want a life filled with happiness, adventure, and opportunity. We all want to enjoy our retirement years surrounded by those we love and doing the things we enjoy. And during the journey toward retirement, we also want peace of mind knowing we're on the right path.

I'll also bet you've complained about taxes at some point during the last 12 months. *"So, what can I do about it?"* you ask yourself. You already work with a team of trusted advisors who help you prepare and pay your taxes each year, right?

Here's the problem with most CPAs when it comes to taxes. They focus all their time on recording the history their clients give them. They put the right numbers in the right boxes on the right forms and get them filed by the right deadlines.

By the time your income tax deadline rolls around each year there isn't much they can tell you other than to put more into your tax-deferred retirement accounts like a 401(k) or IRA.

On the surface, this may sound like sage advice. You'll pay less taxes this year than you would have otherwise, right? (More about this in Chapter 1.)

Have you ever heard of "the law of hammer?" The law of the hammer is a cognitive bias that involves an over-reliance on a familiar tool. As Abraham Maslow said in 1966, *"I suppose it is tempting, if the only tool you have is a hammer, to treat everything as if it were a nail."*

If this is the advice you are getting from your CPA then you may very well have a tax storm gathering.

Stock market risk and burdensome taxes during retirement have created a retirement crisis that has affected the majority of Americans and has probably affected those close to you.

Forbes tells us that we're on the precipice of the greatest retirement crisis in the history of the world. In the decades to come, we will witness millions of elderly Americans, the Baby Boomers, and others, slipping into poverty. Too frail to work, too poor to retire will become the "new normal" for many elderly Americans.

So, you're probably wondering, "Okay, Chris, you've painted the picture. How do I avoid this doomsday scenario with my taxes and future retirement?"

That's a great question and I'm glad you asked. Let's dive into it.

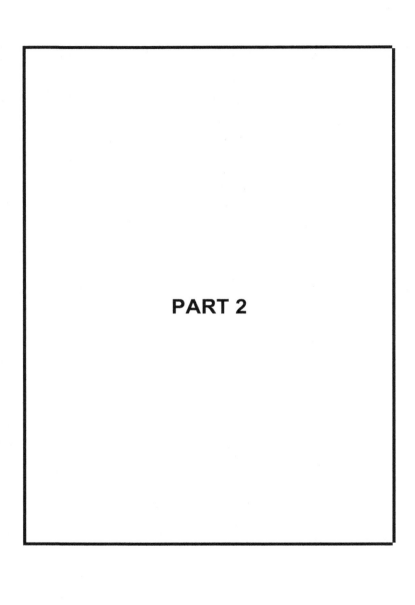

PART 2

# WEALTH BEYOND TAXES

# Chapter 1

# WHY ISN'T MY CPA ALREADY DOING THIS FOR ME?

In today's world, most financially successful pharmaceutical professionals and business owners simply assume that their CPA will bring them innovative tax planning ideas when appropriate to their situation. But that is simply not the case. Traditional CPA firms are asked to do so much and are stretched too thin just trying to produce a compliant tax return or financial statement.

Many CPAs are inundated with smaller clients who generate very little revenue for them and take up a lot of resources. They focus all their time on recording the history a client gives them and putting the right numbers in the right boxes on the right forms and getting that client's tax returns filed by the right deadlines.

But then they call it a day and move on to the next return. By that point, there's not much they can do to change that history (other than encouraging that client to make an occasional 401(k) contribution). So, they don't even try to change it before moving on to the next return.

It's like driving a car using a rear-view mirror instead of looking up the road.  You would never try and back your car out of the garage, back it down the driveway to the street, and back it all the way to work, would you?

But this is the reality of why your CPA typically won't bring you any fresh ideas other than to add more money to your 401(k) or other tax-deferred retirement accounts.

Now, recording history is important, and it's important to do it right. You -- (along with the IRS!) -- want to know how much you make in a year.

But once you hit a certain level of income and taxes, you move beyond wanting to know just how much you owe. **You increasingly want to know how to pay less in taxes.** Unfortunately, most accountants aren't giving that information to you, nor should they, since it really isn't what they do. As we discussed above, their main function is to record your financial history and provide that information to the government.

The reality is that the US Tax code is one of the world's most complicated legal documents with over 150,000 pages and counting. Nobody seems to know how many pages are actually in the current tax code, as it is constantly changing, growing, and becoming more complex.

Now to be fair, CPAs don't spend all their time simply recording history. Plenty of them create year-end projections for their clients. This involves sitting down with a calculator and income statement, estimating how much the client will owe based on the best estimate of those numbers, and adjusting the client's January 15 estimated tax payments up or down based on how those numbers look.

They call that "planning" because it helps clients plan for a bigger or smaller tax bill. And there's real value in planning to avoid an ugly April 15th surprise. But this sort of process isn't really planning at all -- it's projection. The CPAs who do this for their clients are just projecting more scenarios to determine how much the client will eventually owe. And they generally complete the entire exercise without even considering ways to reduce that new, more accurate number.

When you press your CPA for more proactive ways to pay less, this is where they will normally tell you that you should put more money toward your retirement plan -- after all, it will defer the taxes you owe on the money thereby allowing you to pay less taxes immediately. Problem solved, right?

# Chapter 2

# HOW YOUR 401(K) COULD BE A TICKING TAX BOMB

When planning for retirement, the options often discussed are likely familiar: 401(k)s and individual retirement arrangements, known as IRAs.

When information is detailed or hard to process, it's human nature to gravitate toward what we know, and these two savings vehicles are the ones most of us have heard of.

But what is a 401(k) or an IRA? What is a 403(b) or TSP?

These are simply tax codes.

Once we understand that a 401(k) and the like are simply a tool that we can use in saving our money, we then need to understand the tax implications of that tool.

Albert Einstein is quoted as saying that **one of the most complex things in the world is the United States Internal Revenue Code**. So, if that's true, then what we have to understand is that the things we put inside of these tax codes - investments, mutual funds, ETFs, stocks, bonds, real estate, gold, precious metals, Bitcoin, etc. -- these things are ALL subject to taxation depending on the environment in which they are saved.

Retirement plans like 401(k)s, IRAs, and other government plans are designed to postpone the taxes you pay on your earned income. If you are in a higher tax bracket today then when you take it out, you will save money on taxes (you win). If, on the other hand, you are in a lower tax bracket today then when you take it out, you'll pay more taxes (you lose).

If we put our savings into an investment vehicle that defers taxes, we may be very likely hurting ourselves. Why? **Because the U.S. government believes in compound interest as well.**

That is, would you rather pay taxes on the seed (the amount you put in) or on the harvest (the amount you are taking out).

So, the important question becomes whether or not to postpone when you pay taxes.

The truth is, it's easy to answer that question because the evidence is overwhelming. Most people are clearly retiring in higher tax brackets than in their working years. **They are losing the tax game.**

In the late '70s and '80s when retirement plans like the 401(k) started being used, tax brackets were extremely high and were designed to be lower in retirement years. **The tax postponement strategy that worked then is simply not working today.**

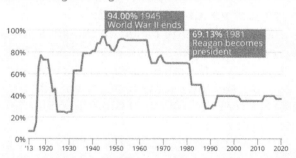

## Taxing The Rich: How America's Marginal Tax Rate Evolved

Historic highest marginal income tax rates in the U.S.*

94.00% 1945
World War II ends

69.13% 1981
Reagan becomes president

* Marginal tax rate is the highest tax rate paid on someone's income and only applies to income over a certain level. - e.g. earnings above $200,000 in 1960 were taxed at 90%.
Source: Tax Policy Center

statista

The majority of Americans are socking money into retirement plans that postpone taxes, which is a poor bet. Across the board, people are retiring with more income and/or lower deductions, and it's truly killing their retirement income.

When you contribute money to a tax-deferred account, it's a bit like going into a business partnership with the IRS. The problem is, every year the IRS gets to vote on what percentage of your profits they get to keep.

So, I have a question for you...

In the future, do you believe taxes will go up, go down or stay the same? We all might have our own opinion on that, but the Congressional Budget Office has already answered that question for us.

**Not only do they say taxes must go up, but they must go up substantially.**

They did a study based on the government's current debt situation, which concluded that with no changes to Social Security, Medicare, and Medicaid, the lowest tax bracket would have to increase by two and a half times in order to sustain those programs.

Here's the really bad news. They also said that the 25% bracket would rise to 63% and the highest bracket, 39.6% would need to rise to 88%. Can you imagine 88% of your nest egg going to the IRS in taxes? That's a risk I'm not willing to take with my life savings.

# Chapter 3

# WHAT MATTERS MOST TO YOU?

As we discussed in Chapter 1 *Why Isn't My CPA Already Doing This For Me?* you are likely being advised by your CPA that the way to pay less tax (this year!) is to put more money in your tax-deferred retirement accounts.

And as we discussed in Chapter 2 *How Your 401(k) Could Be a Ticking Tax Bomb*, you are already likely working with an advisor or money manager who is tasked with getting you the best rate of return for your stock portfolio inside of your tax-deferred accounts like your 401(k) or IRA.

Nothing wrong with that. That is very typical for most people.

One of the things that I've learned in my career is that there are rules that financial institutions such as banks typically know, but most regular investors don't.

The way I like to illustrate this is, "Have you ever played a game of tic-tac-toe?"

Who won the game the first time you played it? Most likely, the person who introduced you to the game. The person who showed you how to play the game.

"You want to play tic-tac-toe, three in a row?" They likely won.

Your CPA, while likely an excellent accountant and a nice person, and someone who you should trust when it comes to filing your yearly tax returns and paying your quarterly estimates, is likely not the best person to get advice from on how to significantly pay less taxes over the course of your lifetime.

Likewise, your money manager is likely not a retirement-income specialist. Instead, he is likely narrowly focused on managing your money, keeping your focus on average rates of return your portfolio is earning. It's not his role to show you how to maximize your income in retirement. He just wants to help you climb to the top of the mountain.

But retirement is not about just getting to the top of the mountain. It's about getting back down the mountain or living until the end of your life without having to sacrifice your lifestyle out of uncertainty and fear.

**So what else should you be thinking about when it comes to planning for retirement?**

Everyone is different, and your goals are uniquely your own. So when it comes to defining goals, here are the six most common priorities people have.

**Income**, a.k.a. cash flow, a.k.a money you can spend. This means that when you go into retirement your role has changed from that of an accumulator to that of a spender, and the purpose of your wealth is to provide you with income/cash flow that you can spend. It is not a reflection or commentary on the type of investor personality you may associate with (i.e., Safety/ Income/ Growth/ Aggressive Growth). It merely indicates that Income of some amount is a requirement from your accumulated wealth in order to meet your spending needs that are not covered by Social Security, pension, or other sources.

**Growth** is a priority whereby you ensure that the focus of your portfolio is to appreciate in value, understanding that with potential growth comes the potential risk of loss. In my experience, many times the person will want to and be willing to dial down the market risk in their portfolio and from the overall planning perspective generally. The reason many people include Growth in their priorities in retirement is to enable their income to keep pace with inflation. Alternatively, for funds not needed for their own retirement income, investing them for growth may result in more money left for the beneficiaries and thus be a legacy motivation.

**Preservation** means *"Don't lose my money!"*. Or, as Will Rogers once said, *"I am more concerned with the return of my money than a return on my money"*. For purposes of our discussion, it means that to some degree a person is not willing to accept a loss in exchange for a higher rate of return. The person for whom preservation is a priority will focus more of their plan on guaranteed principal assets. Preservation does not have to be absolute. Frequently, the plan designed with a client will result in x% of the assets being protected from investment risk.

**Liquidity.** That sum of money which is easily accessible by you, at a moment's notice. Most of the time, people think of this as cash in the bank, but it could be "stored" in other types of accounts as well. The point is that a specific sum of cash is readily accessible. For some people, this number is reflective of a certain number of months of household operating cash flow. For others, it includes a reserve for maintenance and repairs on the house, like hot water heaters, a/c systems, etc.

**Heirs & Beneficiaries.** As the name implies, H & B refers to the financial and other resource benefits you wish to leave for other people you love when you die. For families with young children, Heirs and Beneficiaries is much higher on the list. For older clients, Heirs & Beneficiaries will typically be lower on the list. For older clients with special-needs children and/or those whose objectives include legacy for children or grandchildren, H&B would be higher on the list. Almost always, those with wealth in excess of what they will spend in their own lifetimes seek to maximize what stays in the family.

**Debt.** In addition to taxes, debt is one of the biggest destroyers of wealth. From a planning perspective, figuring out how to eliminate personal debt quickly will greatly accelerate the wealth-creation process.

# Chapter 4

# WHAT THE WEALTHY KNOW ABOUT RISK AND TAXES

Warren Buffet, one of the greatest investors of our day, subscribes to the following philosophy when it comes to investing.

*"Rule number one is to never lose money. Rule number two is to never forget rule number one."*

I agree! And if you do too, then you'll love what you are about to learn in this chapter.

Let's take a brief journey back in time....

In October of 1929, the stock market suffered severe losses. It plunged over 22% in just a few short days, making headlines across the country. Over the next several years, the markets would have difficulty recovering. The Dow Jones

Industrial Average would take a staggering 32-year setback, losing nearly 90% of its value.

From its peak of 381.17 in September 1929, it would close at a shocking 41.22 on July 8, 1932. It would take another 22 years to surpass its all-time high before the crash of 1929.

During that period of time:

Nearly 25% of all Americans would be unemployed and unable to find work.

Over 40% of banks would shut down.

Millions of savings accounts would simply disappear.

But in the midst of all that devastation, there was a silver lining for some people.

Life insurance companies remained virtually unaffected during that tumultuous time. More importantly, while the market suffered severe losses, **the policy owners of cash value life insurance didn't lose a dime!**

That's such an important point, let me say it again.

During the Great Depression, arguably one of the worst periods of economic disaster our country has ever been through, those who had invested in cash value life insurance policies didn't lose a dime!

In fact, cash value life insurance was such a stable place to have money that while many people lost everything those who owned cash value life insurance were even paid profits in every single year of the Great Depression![1]

Fast forward to our present time. With out-of-control government spending and debt and our world being radically reshaped both politically and economically as a result of the coronavirus pandemic, knowing how and where to keep your money safe (and out of reach of the IRS!) is becoming increasingly important.

## Banks and Corporations

While many wealthy individuals maximize the use of cash value life insurance, there is one specific group that really understands its value. This same sector of the economy controls nearly every aspect of our economy.

Cash-value life insurance plays a massive role in financial institutions, corporations, and banks. These organizations buy life insurance by the billions, and use it for many different reasons.

Not only does it increase their financial stability and reduce their taxes, but it is also an ideal place to fund employee pensions, healthcare costs, and other benefits.

The FDIC makes available the balance sheets of nearly
every major bank. The following figures are directly from
FDIC.gov and represent the exact amount of money the following banks hold in life insurance.

| Bank | Life Insurance Assets |
|---|---|
| Bank of America | $19,607,000,000 |
| Wells Fargo Bank | $17,739,000,000 |
| JP Morgan Chase Bank | $10,327,000,000 |
| U.S. Bank | $5,451,892,000 |

Banks are in the business of money. They have some of the greatest minds in the world, including economists, attorneys, accountants, financial analysts, and other experts helping them increase the efficiency and use of their capital.

It is not insignificant that banks place billions of dollars in life insurance. It's a reflection of the value they place on this powerful asset. For banks, it provides the ultimate in safety, stability, and growth.

Corporations are also heavily involved in investing heavily in cash value life insurance. It is also significant to note that these corporations rely heavily on life insurance to fund an employee's retirement plan and their top executives' retirement plans.

Among its many benefits, the ability of cash value life insurance to provide the stable growth necessary to create a predictable income is one of its most powerful features.

Here is a list of some well-known companies that hold cash value life insurance as an asset[2]:

- Starbucks
- Johnson & Johnson
- Pfizer
- Verizon
- Comcast
- Walt Disney
- Lockheed Martin

- Nike
- CVS
- Bed, Bath & Beyond
- General Electric

In the 1900s, it's estimated that over 50% of savings went into cash value life insurance.[3] It was the staple for safety, protection, and predictable future income for decades.

Today, Americans are being told by Wall Street and others with vested interests that volatile, risk-based investing in the stock market is the best way to prepare for retirement.

*"Why would they do that?"* you may be asking. You see, Wall Street investment firms were a big part of how government plans like 401(k)s got established in the first place. These elite insiders positioned themselves to be the managers of the funds that ultimately made their way into these plans. There have been many books that go into much greater detail about this phenomenon. Suffice it to say here that there has been a massive transition for the worse from safety and guarantees to risky, unpredictable stock market investments.

Thousands of Americans are starting to see the outcomes of these failed models, and are looking for a better path.

---

[1] Patch, B. W. (1933). Life insurance in the depression. *Editorial research reports 1933* (Vol. I). http://library.cqpress.com/cqresearcher/cqresrre1933051900

[2] Dyke, Barry James. "CORPORATE-OWNED LIFE INSURANCE." The Pirates of Manhattan: Systematically Plundering the American Consumer & How to Protect against it. Portsmouth, NH: 555 Publishing. 2007.174-176. Print.

[3] Thompson, Jake. "Money. Wealth. Life Insurance." Jake Thompson. 2013. 14. Print.

# Chapter 5

# A MORE TAX EFFICIENT SAVINGS STRATEGY

Cash value life insurance is one of the most tax-friendly financial tools we have. Money inside cash value life insurance, when handled properly, grows tax-free, can be used tax-free, and passes on tax-free.

## "But I Can Get A Better Return In The Stock Market"

You might think the point of this section is to try and convince you that you can't get better returns, but it's not.

I strongly believe that conventional forms of investing -- especially stocks and mutual funds --

will fall far short of what a solid cash value policy will do with much less risk. And that's not even the most important aspect of cash value life insurance.

One of the most important benefits of cash value life insurance is your guaranteed access to your money at any time you want it. If you feel you can get better returns somewhere else, and you're willing to take the risk, the insurance policy will actually make the investment more profitable.

For example, imagine you have money in a life insurance policy. And also imagine you have an opportunity to go in on a time-sensitive real estate investment. You are convinced that this real estate investment will pay you DOUBLE-DIGIT returns consistently for a number of years to come. That's fantastic! You can easily access the money inside your cash value life insurance policy to fund the real estate investment.

Conversely, if you had your money tied up in a government retirement plan, you would likely not have been able to take advantage of this opportunity without being penalized and being taxed!

**Tax-free growth**

Among many benefits, I believe the most attractive benefit of cash value life insurance is the way it is taxed. This benefit alone attracts those that want protection from the uncertainty of taxes.

Let's talk about a few of those tax benefits.

The first, and arguably one of the most important, is tax-free growth.

How is this possible?

Growth inside of some insurance policies is called a dividend, and by definition, is considered a "return of premium." Since the IRS considers this a return of what you have already paid, it is not taxable. In other policies, growth is called a credit and because of tax codes 72e and 7702 no income tax is due when you access this cash value.

That being said, there is one caveat to this; as the policy grows, you will have undoubtedly accumulated more than you contributed if you've designed your policy for high cash value. If at any point you decide to withdraw your money from the insurance policy, the growth (everything above the cost basis of the policy) can be taxable.

However, as long as you keep the policy intact, **it will continue to grow tax-free indefinitely.** And as you'll soon discover, there is practically no reason to ever cancel the policy, keeping those dollars tax-free for the rest of your life.

The appeal of tax-free growth on your money is one of the biggest reasons large organizations and savvy individuals pump millions of dollars into these policies each year. You'll have a hard time finding a better place for these types of tax benefits.

### Tax-free Death Benefit

When you've amassed a large amount of wealth over the course of your lifetime, there's only one thing that stands in the way of passing the benefit of that hard work on to your family...Uncle Sam!

In my view, the death tax is unfair, inefficient, economically unsound, and, frankly, immoral.

Whether you have a big estate or a small estate, passing on money can be painful. Some of the largest estates are stripped to nearly nothing after taxes and probate. It is estimated that the death tax causes one-third of all family-owned small businesses to liquidate after the death of the owner.

Would you like some good news?

In addition to the tax-free growth, which we outlined in the last section, cash value life insurance provides a tax-free death benefit to your loved ones.

This means your life insurance death benefit will transfer with no income tax to those you choose to leave it to.

I can assure you of one thing: there is no better asset to die with than life insurance. It is the most heavily used estate planning tool in the country because it can help pass on more of your hard-earned money to your family.

# Chapter 6

# SUPERCHARGING YOUR RETIREMENT WITH A LIRP

I f you are between the ages of 45 to 65, you are likely more acutely aware of how well you have (or haven't!) saved for retirement.

To compensate, it may be helpful to avail yourself of another tool I oftentimes recommend to clients to use the tax code to their advantage to maximize their income and wealth, especially in retirement: the *Life Insurance Retirement Plan* (LIRP).

A LIRP life insurance policy that is specifically designed to maximize cash value accumulation. At the same time, it is designed to minimize the death benefit because the goal isn't the death benefit but the tax advantages it affords you while you are living.

I recall from *Chapter 4 What the Wealthy Know About Risk*, corporations rely heavily on life insurance to fund an employee's retirement plan and their top executives' retirement plans. It should come as no surprise that about 85% of the CEOs of Fortune 500 companies utilize the LIRP as one of their primary retirement tools.

In addition to its tax-free benefits, the LIRP provides a compelling array of options for growing dollars within the tax-free accumulation account.

For example, you can do the following:

1. You can opt to grow your money within the general investment portfolio of the insurance company that administers the program. Because insurance companies are in the business of managing risk, these types of returns tend to be conservative, but very consistent.
2. You can pass your contributions through insurance companies into mutual fund portfolios called sub-accounts. While this approach can provide much higher returns,

it does expose you to the impact of market declines.

3. You can contribute dollars to an accumulation account whose growth is linked to the upward movement of a stock market index like the S&P 500. You can participate in the growth of this index up to a cap, typically 11% and 13%. On the flip side, **if the index ever loses money, the account is credited zero so it actually never goes down in value.** With back-tested historical returns between 7% and 9%, this can be a safe but productive way to accumulate tax-free dollars for retirement.

One of my favorite features that some LIRPs can include is **leverage.**

Studies show that your retirement will likely cost you an average of 6 times more than your house. And if you are like most people, you have probably used financing to live in a better house than you would have otherwise been able to afford if you had to pay for the house in cash.

Similarly, Kaizen® is a unique life insurance tool that uses leverage and provides you an opportunity to earn significantly more interest while at the same time eliminating the risk of market decline.

What is revolutionary about Kaizen® is that it is the only strategy that provides you the opportunity to add up to 3 times more money using other people's money.

As a result of this leverage, you have the potential for an additional 60-100% of tax-free income in retirement, and without the typical risks associated with leverage.

**"Why Haven't I Ever Heard of Kaizen®?"**

Historically, Kaizen, and other forms of LIRPs have been reserved for the wealthiest segment of America's population.  It wasn't until recently that companies began to re-engineer these programs to mimic the Roth IRA. They knew if they could structure the LIRP to capture the tax-free qualities of the Roth IRA, **but without the accumulation limitations**, they would significantly benefit the everyday saver who was looking to maximize their tax-free income.

Is Kaizen® the right strategy for you? As a fiduciary, I can't answer that question here. It depends on your unique circumstances and goals. If Kaizen does sound interesting to you, you can check out the following website so that you can learn more about it.

https://www.myilia.com/kaizen Feel free to reach out to me with any questions about Kaizen®. You can reach me at Chris@ProfessionalPlanningServices.com

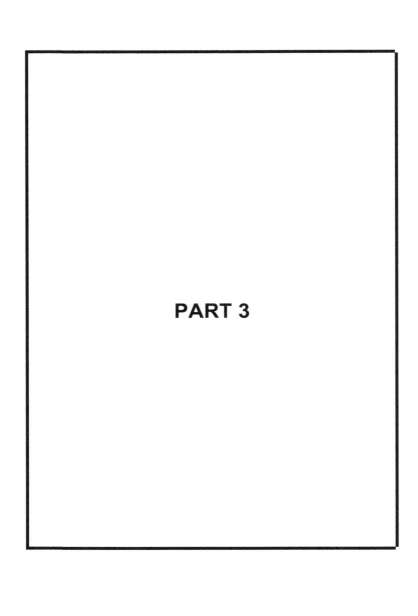

PART 3

# THE PATH FORWARD

# 7 QUESTIONS YOU NEED ANSWERED TO PROPERLY PLAN FOR RETIREMENT

This book, while intentionally small, is about big ideas. My goal has been to help you begin the exciting process of totally transforming the way you plan for your future retirement by leveraging the tax code to your advantage.

The #1 problem I've identified in my 30 years as a financial planner is that dated strategies of maxing out 401(k)s or IRAs and utilizing a traditional 60/40 split for asset allocation just isn't going to work anymore.

I don't want you to just REACH retirement, I want you to have enough income and wealth to thrive!

Toward that end, you should know the answers to the following 7 questions... and if your advisor can't give them to you, you should fire them. Even if that advisor is you.

So, ask yourself, do you know the answers to these questions?

## Do you know the rate of return you may need for you to live like you live today and have your money last?

My experience is that most people want to maintain their current lifestyle when they retire. Think of it like this: retiring could equate to being on unemployment...but for 30 years.

You've probably heard these 30 years referred to as 3 separate ten-year periods... "the go-go years," "the slow-go years," and "the no-go years." During these periods, having your money keep up with your desired lifestyle (including inflation), is not an easy feat.

You may have heard what I like to refer to as the "broken rule" from your human resource department or 401k, 403b, or TSP advisors -– "You only need 75% of your income in retirement." That advice is questionable. Your advisor or human resources representative never takes into account one of the greatest risks in retirement called "Sequence of Return Risk." In essence what that means is that if your existing retirement plan is using an average rate of return to forecast your probability of success, you may very well learn the hard way that averages lie.

## Do you know how much you need to save each year to make sure you will have enough?

Quite simply, I show this figure to my clients last. The reason for that is because the answer is almost always depressing. I have learned that most folks will spend more time researching a 2-week vacation than they will learning about the nuances of retirement (also depressing, to some).

Retirement differs from when we are working because we turn off our income... that's it. No one can predict (*let alone wants to think about!*) when they will die. But if you're not planning for 30-40 years of retirement (and saving accordingly), you could find out in the later stages of life that a miscalculation can lead to an undesirable lifestyle.

For example, no one wants to pack up their most prized possessions and go to a nursing home. Put simply, nursing homes are depressing and carry the stigma that they are a place where you go to die. But what happens when someone exhausts all their resources and has not planned properly for an end-of-life event necessitating long-term care? The answer is devastating –- they could become a ward of the state and that's never pretty.

**Do you know how long you will have to work before you can stop and have your money last to your life expectancy?**

It's one thing being able to retire and work or consult at your leisure... but it's another thing to either HAVE to continue working or to be forced to STOP working due to an illness or disease.

I have seen folks retire after working their entire lives, only to have their health prevent them from living the golden years we all dream of.

Even worse, I have seen folks pass away too soon, never expecting that they would become ill. Hug the ones you're with, make time for your family, and plan for the golden years to be just that: golden.

Too many financial advisors are narrowly focused on the rate of return of a portfolio instead of the quality of life that is desired.

**Do you know how much you may need to reduce your future lifestyle to keep from running out of money?**

This goes back to the 1st question and a myth that has circulated in the pre-retiree community for years. Why would someone want to live on 20-30% less than what they are living on now?

My job as a retirement income specialist is to help you maintain 100% of your current lifestyle while at the same time helping you safeguard that plan against unforeseen events. It's OK to make cutbacks in situations that call for it. But why intentionally design a 30% reduction in your lifestyle if you can avoid it?

## Does your portfolio have cancer?

I know the "C" word is serious, ominous, and extreme. That is the reason I chose it. If you had cancer, would you want to know? I, for one, would, and I hope I never get it. It's an ugly disease.

Well, when your portfolio has cancer and no one has taken steps to eradicate it, you could find yourself with a lot less money than you had anticipated. What's this cancer called? Taxes!

I regularly speak with a lot of very educated individuals who you would think would have figured this out. But it's not intuitive.

What do I mean? Let me ask you these questions: Do you contribute to an IRA or 401K, 403b, or TSP (*these are all tax-deferred plans*)? I almost always get a 100% affirmation that they are not only participating in but investing as much as possible in these plans.

So, if this is true for you, the next question I ask is this: Do you think income taxes in this country will be lower (as you were probably told initially) the same or higher when you retire? 100% of the folks I ask this question to answer, "Higher!"

I hate to break the news to you, but if you answered the same and think you can save money in a rising tax environment, this makes no mathematical sense.

To clarify, If I could have paid .25 cents on $1 today and possibly .33, .40, .50, or even .70 cents tax on that dollar in the future, you're making a HUGE miscalculation.

I understand folks do this because this is the advice everyone, including their CPAs and tax advisors and their human resources and employers are giving them...but the rules have changed and are changing very quickly still, and taking steps to eradicate this cancer is prudent.

## Do you have a portfolio or a plan?

As a financial planner, I have learned not to idolize tools. Most people view their portfolios as the solution, when in fact it's just part of what they should be considering. It's not the fault of most people, though.

For years major insurance companies and financial institutions have bombarded us with commercials with the message: "What's your number?" as folks walk around with this sum of money over their head. What a misleading commercial. Getting to retirement with a sum of money should not be the goal. Getting through retirement with enough assets, income, and desired lifestyle, would be a better strategy.

Retirement is not about how much money you have amassed, but instead, it's about identifying your income needs based on your specific criteria, and then figuring out if all of your assets will help generate enough supplemental income to meet your needs.

Remember this mantra: Retirement is about income, it's about income, it's about income.

## What's your Sharpe Ratio?

Most people have never heard of Sharpe Ratio – and many don't know how it affects their portfolio. The formula for Sharpe Ratio is defined as the risk-free rate of return –- the average rate of return divided by standard deviation equals the Sharpe Ratio. In plain English, the formula for Sharpe Ratio answers the question "are you being rewarded enough for the amount of risk you are taking?"

Most folks have more risk in their portfolio than they know, and to make matters worse, they believe they are diversified, when in fact they are in investments like mutual funds and other holdings which quite often are identical across the board.

So now that you know the questions that you should be asking, what can you do right now to better prepare for the future? The answer is simple: get a second opinion.

If there are holes in your financial cruise ship, when do you want to be made aware? When it's still salvageable, or after the ship is taking on water and it's too far gone to save?

If you found that you didn't have the answers to the questions above, and you'd like help answering them, I want to invite you to take...

# Chapter 8

# THE NEXT STEP

*"It's not what you know; it's not even who you know; it's what you implement that counts."*

Congratulations! You are one step closer to having the peace of mind that comes from knowing that you are on the right path to enjoying a retirement filled with happiness, adventure, and opportunity.

Imagine what it will feel like to know that both your future, that of your family, and your legacy are secure.

Trust me, it's gratifying and makes the entire planning process worthwhile.

As I said earlier, I wrote this book for two primary reasons: 1) to help, inform and motivate pharmaceutical professionals like you; 2) to extend an invitation to see if working together to help you create more income and wealth makes sense -- for both of us.

If you like what you have read so far and feel that working directly with me to either create or improve your retirement plan makes sense, let me ask you to consider these three questions:

1. Do you believe taxes will go up in the future?
2. Are you serious and committed to using the tax code to your advantage legally, morally, and ethically, so that you and your family can create more income and wealth for years (*even generations!*) to come?
3. Do you value working with an expert to guide you, bring out the best in you, and prevent mistakes?

If your answers are three affirmations, then, as I see it, you have two pathways in front of you at this very moment in time.

1.  You can close this book and do nothing with the information I shared. (If you have gotten this far, I surely hope this is not an option.)
2.  You can schedule a 15-minute introductory phone call with me to begin the conversation on how we might work together.

If you are serious about your financial future, you have nothing to lose by choosing the second pathway.

This one phone call may hold the key to unlocking the door to your peace of mind knowing that you are on the right path to enjoying a retirement filled with happiness, adventure, and opportunity.

There is no obligation, and scheduling it is super easy.

I understand your goals are uniquely yours, which is why you and I need to talk -- if you are serious about implementing any of the ideas in this book.

This call is all about helping you decide if working together is a good fit for both of us. Maybe we are meant to work together. Maybe not. But we will not know unless you and I have this first, critical conversation.

## Note: It's NOT a Sales Call

It's a two-way interview to make sure we agree this is a good match. I'll ask you some questions, and you can ask me some questions (in fact, as many questions as you want). And then, we can go from there.

This is typically a 15-minute phone call; however, we will stay on until you're satisfied you are ready to work with me or you simply want to move on. That's it. There is no obligation on your part.

I am a firm believer that everyone should be working with certain people -- not everybody -- but people who "get" you and understand what's most important to you and your family.

I feel the same way about the people whom I work with, and in order for us to see if we are a good fit, I have found these calls to be the ideal litmus test. It will give us a chance to "meet" and see if working together makes sense.

TODAY Is the Day. NOW Is the Time.

Schedule your **Wealth Beyond Taxes Strategy Session** with me right now. There's absolutely no fee, no obligation, no risk, and nothing to lose.

How to Schedule Our Call:

Go to https://calendly.com/chrisjlester/15-minute-call
and pick a day and time that works best for you. That's it! Or if you have any questions you can email me directly at
chris@professionalplanningservices.com

I look forward to hearing from you, and more importantly, working together to help you create more income and wealth for you and your family for years to come!

# RESOURCES & SOCIAL MEDIA

In addition to the resources I have already shared with you throughout this book here are a few more that you can check out.

My Website:
https://www.professionalplanningservices.com/

My LinkedIn:
https://www.linkedin.com/in/chris-lester-nj/

My YouTube Channel:
https://www.youtube.com/channel/UCOXdg8ILZY1jQALgoS9DatA

# ABOUT CHRIS LESTER [VIDEO INTERVIEW]

I'm the President and founder of Professional Planning Services, Inc. and Education Funding Specialists, LLC. in Somerset, New Jersey, and an Investment Advisor Representative with Retirement Wealth Advisors, Inc. (RWA), an SEC Registered Investment Advisor. I also own a tax preparation company called EZ Pro-Tax, dedicated to helping families review their financial efficiency in partnership with an experienced CPA.

I am a United States Navy veteran and my training in mechanical engineering gives me an inherent ability to problem solve. I hold the Chartered Financial Consultant (ChFC®) designation, the Retirement Income Certified

Professional (RICP®) designation, and Certified College Planner (CCPS) designation.

I am a partner of the Eagle Team Financial Pros. This is a nationwide training organization of advisors, CPA's and attorneys that share a holistic approach when dealing with clients vs. a product-driven conversation. I am also a Master Mentor of the Money-Trax system Circle of Wealth. As a mentor and trainer, I personally produce as well as help advisors across the country with their client's unique situations. I have helped 1000's of families across the nation by analyzing their current plans to retire and then improve upon retirement finances so they can thrive all the way through retirement.

I am a member of the New Jersey Better Business Bureau. I am married with four children and live in Cream Ridge, New Jersey. I'm an accomplished 4th-degree black belt in Isshin-Ryu karate and I train in Brazilian Jiu-Jitsu and Wing Chun Kung Fu.

In addition, **I find that video is a great medium to get to know someone.**

Toward that end, I created this 15-minute video so you can get to know me a bit better and determine if you think we might be a good fit.

Here is the link to the 15-minute video.
https://bit.ly/meetchrislester

I've included the transcript of the recording below for those who prefer to simply read.

### Transcript

**Question:**
Tell me a little bit about the process of working with you. Someone's read this book. They're interested. They want to know how to engage you. **How do they engage you and what does that process look like?** What can they expect from that process?

**Chris Lester:**

In doing this for 30 years and being in a partnership with a group of advisors that helps oversee other advisors, **I've learned that people are tired of being sold.** I just had a phone call with somebody and they said that they had talked to three other advisors and it very quickly turned into this sales type of phone call or meeting.

I have elected to have a neutral meeting arrangement, which is, I will build a model, which is what I deem "you are here." It requires some sharing of information, but nothing sensitive, nothing specific. I don't need social security numbers. I don't need tax returns yet. I don't need account numbers or even the account statements yet.

**Chris Lester:**

But I do want a high-level understanding. **What I do that most advisors don't do is I really ask them to drill down onto the expense arena.** Now, let's be honest. Most people don't like to look at their expenses. Nobody wants to look at the skeletons in their closets. Some families, they're very good. They have QuickBooks. They have an

Excel spreadsheet. They have all that data at their fingertips, and it's not a big deal. But with some folks, it's a little gray. The left hand doesn't necessarily know what the right hand's spending.

Because there's, typically, in a household, there's one person that's in charge of the bills or certain funds and the other person, I hear this quite often, which is, *"Oh, if they say it's okay, it's okay with me."*

That's fine, but **when it comes to planning, especially long-term planning, we need to start to ask some of the tougher questions.** Not just what are you doing now? This is where my experience comes in. I hold a designation, Retirement Income Certified Planner. That designation is a very high-level skill set, which not only helps families get to retirement, but through retirement, and that is a very distinct difference. I've taught classes over at Rutgers, at the business school. **When I poll the audiences there, I'll say how many people here in the audience are afraid of running out of money in their retirement, and almost a resounding yes. Everybody has that fear**.

If you follow traditional wisdom, and I don't

necessarily mean traditional wisdom. What I really mean is if you follow **traditional marketing advice from the financial institutions, what they will tout is that you need to have some sum of money by age 65, and you'll be fine. We have found that, because of the risks that are associated with retirement, that that can actually be devastating, critically wrong advice.** Because, again, there are things called sequence of return risks. There are longevity risks. There are risks that happen in retirement that we aren't facing when we're working. I have some idioms or some expressions that I've shared or developed over the years.

The first is, it's **when you get to retirement and your last day of work is like now being on unemployment for the next 20, 30, maybe even 40 years.** Will your money last? If you use some traditional models, like the 4% rule that could actually end up being very costly to you and your family, because you could find, at 75, that now you're not as wealthy as you thought you were. The second thing that I have is I say, *"When you get to retirement, we have to segment the timeframe."* Let's say, and I know a lot of people say, *"Oh, I'm*

70

*not going to live that long,"* or, *"Retiring and I'll collect social security at 65 or 67 or 87."* Everybody's got an answer. I'm not saying that your logic is flawed. But what I say is that are we thinking about things clearly?

Let's imagine that we have, at age 65, we decide that we're going to retire for 30 years. 30 years, you have **the first 10 years is what I call the go-go years**. We have our health. We have our money. We have our sanity. We've now hung up our cleats and we're ready to retire. We want to travel. We want to see the world. We want to spend time with the kids and the grandkids. Well, we can do that.

**Then, we have what we call the slow-go years.** The slow-go years, now we have to slow down a little bit because maybe we don't have that skip in our step. We don't have that desire. Maybe we've gotten injured or maybe we're just happy spending time with the family close by. And then, we have the no-go years. I'm not going anywhere. My knees hurt. My back hurts. I can't get out of bed. I'm going to stay right here and anybody that wants to come to see me can come to visit.

We call it the go-go, the slow-go, and the no-go

years. As you're speaking with folks, when you're 45 and you're making a lot of money and you have young children and you're trying to get these kids' homework done and everything that's going on. And then, at 55, oh my God, 10 years until I retire, **it's this spot, from about 45 to 65, that I help to start to say with a plan, we can start to help stack the odds in your favor.**

That's why I'm so passionate about what I do is because I've helped a lot of families. I just had a call today with a family, significant wealth, that I've helped them over the last 10 years put three kids through college. He ended up losing his job last year at 55 years old. Nothing gave me greater, greater comfort to be able to say that you're going to be fine. You have very little chance of running out of money. And then, he got a new job and everything's now rosy.

I mean, that's what happens when life happens. Unbeknownst to us, what could happen in the real world? Could be a death, could be a divorce, could be a failed business, could be a loss of job employment, or maybe we just decide we want to hang up our cleats and maybe pursue another career, and we have to be prepared for the unexpected. That's why dealing with a seasoned veteran, I think, is so critically important and it's my skill set.

**Question**
You've been doing this for 30 years and, before that, you were in the Navy, I believe?

**Chris Lester:**
Yes, sir.

**Question**
Just looking back on your career, whether it's in terms of what you do now or just key lessons, **what are maybe one or two key insights or lessons that you've learned as a person or in working with people that you've learned along the way?**

**Chris Lester:**
Wow, that's a quick question with a lengthy answer. **I went into the Navy at a very young age to be Navy SEAL.** My uncle was Navy SEAL and I wanted to pursue in his footsteps, wanted to serve my country, and I signed on the dotted line. I went

in and I actually had volunteered to go into BUD/S and was getting ready, and I had my vision tests and my eyesight was not up to par. It was beyond the ability to be corrected, so I was not able to participate in BUD/S.

I learned a couple of things in the military, A, a work ethic. My Uncle Ron, who was a Navy SEAL, always said this, *"Whatever you're going to try, a lot of people want to try things, do it for a year."* If you can do it for at least a year, then you've given it a fair assessment on whether it works or not.

**Part of that passion has developed and stemmed over into the martial arts**. I am a martial artist. I am a ranked black belt in Isshin-Ryu karate. I also train in Brazilian jujitsu, Japanese jujitsu, and Wing Chun. I have two younger girls. They're 14, and my youngest actually turned 12 yesterday. I train them and they train with other instructors every night. I believe that... **I'm a huge proponent of women's self-defense, that you have to expect the unexpected.**

I want us all to be happy and safe, and I hope everything turns out well. But when I went into the Navy, my best friend was hit by a drunk driver and broke his neck and he's been in a wheelchair ever since.

I learned at a very young age how fragile we are and how fragile life is. All I try and do and part of, I guess, **my philosophy has been to make somebody's life better, some way shape, or form, just in dealing with me. But I have an expression. I am not going to tell you what you want to hear, but I am going to tell you what you need to know.** And so, sometimes, I try not to be too intense all the time.

I like to have a good time, but my family's important to me. Spending time with the people that we care about, and I say this all the time. I do a weekly chat with Chris, and I've been saying this for a couple of years now, hug the ones you're with because life is so short and we just never know when today's going to be our last day.

When I'm working with families and I'm sensing that there's help that I can offer, quite often I'm not even compensated for some of the advice that I give and that's okay. **I am a fiduciary so sometimes people... I had that question yesterday, are you a fiduciary? Absolutely. The Reader's Digest version of what that means, I**

**must, by law, put somebody's interests ahead of my own**. But my interests and hobbies are broad. I scuba dive. I like to dive with sharks, not because I'm a risk-taker, but just because I think they're amazing creatures. My oldest son scuba dives with me. We have been blessed with, pre-COVID, to go to some pretty cool places and check out some things. I also enjoy riding a Harley, to be able to do that. Again, I wish I could do it a little bit more, but New Jersey, it's hard to drive safely and I like to be on the open road.

I still practice, daily, martial arts. I like that. I like movies. I like movies with the family. Disney is one of our favorite places on the planet and we're going there in February. These are just things about me if people were saying, *"Hey, who is Chris Lester?"* I'm a person that's been around the block, grew up in New Jersey, understands all the nonsense that typically can happen here. I just try to help you to understand, A, what you have, B, once you understand what you have and now that you know that there are other options, is that what you want? And then, from there, **most of my clients, at the end of the day, I can say this and I'm proud of this, become my**

**friends**. I'm not a fit for everybody. That's okay. But **the people that I do work with, I think I've helped to make their lives a little better and that's important to me.**

**Question:**
Final question... Is there any question that I haven't asked that you would like to speak about or address?

**Chris Lester:**
**My family's important. People are important. I cannot say that enough.** I'm 57 now. I lost my dad at 54. This year I've seen two high school buddies I went to school with pass away. I've had two advisors that have passed away. One was 58, the other was 65, and not from COVID. None of them passed from COVID. As I go through this journey that we call life, I reflect on how I'm very blessed to be alive. I feel very fortunate to be able to have and have built a lifestyle that, I think, my family appreciates me. I'm able to provide for them. I'm able to offer guidance and wisdom, not just to my family, but to other families.

As I go through this, I think it's nice to be able

to, ultimately, and I use this term like, "Hey, I'm a financial advisor. **As a fiduciary. I have to disclose, I get paid how I get paid." All that stuff will come up over time. But my goal is... If you said, "What is your goal in the relationship of helping a family?" It's to elevate myself to that trusted advisor category.** That's where I feel I have dialed in because if somebody is picking up the phone to say, *"Hey, I'm thinking about buying a new car. How should I pay for this? Should I lease it? Should I finance it?"* That I have enough of a relationship with that family that I can help them make thoughtful decisions.

Somebody is saying, *"Hey, listen, I'm thinking about giving some money away for charity. What's the best way to do that? Should we set up a will and a trust, powers of attorney?"* I just have a female client now. Her beneficiaries are in another country. And so, it's just being able to help people to have a good, thoughtful sounding board that, quite often, I got no horse in this race. It's just giving, based on my experience, my professional opinions, and I love sharing and I love helping. **At the end of the day, that's what gives me a lot of** joy is helping other families to be able to make it through this journey of life.

# SERVICES

In addition to the ideas and strategies detailed in this book, here is a comprehensive list of the services I offer:

- Term Insurance
- Financial and Wealth Planning
- Health Insurance
- Investment Management
- Kaizen
- Legacy Planning
- Lifebridge
- Results in Advance Planning
- Retirement Income Planning
- Roth Conversion Strategies
- Social Security Maximization

- Tax Strategies
- Disability Insurance
- Medicare Supplemental Insurance
- Permanent Life Insurance

You can learn more and get the most up to date information at my website at:
https://www.professionalplanningservices.com/

# Disclosures

Brookstone Disclosure - Investment advisory services offered through Brookstone Wealth Advisors, LLC (BWA), a registered investment advisor. BWA and Professional Planning Services are independent of each other. Insurance products and services are not offered through BWA but are offered and sold through individually licensed and appointed agents.

Fiduciary Disclosure: Registered Investment Advisors and Investment Advisor Representatives act as fiduciaries for all of our investment management clients. We have an obligation to act in the best interests of our clients and to make full disclosure of any conflicts of interests, if any exist. Please refer to our firm brochure, the ADV 2A page 4, for additional information.

Insurance Guarantee Disclosure - Any comments regarding safe and secure investments, and guaranteed income streams refer only to fixed insurance products. They do not refer, in any way to securities or investment advisory products. Fixed Insurance and Annuity product guarantees are subject to the claims-paying ability of the issuing company and are not offered by BWA.

14780765R00055